A POCKET GUIDE TO THE LIFE AND MEANING OF JESUS

Also published by Mowbray

A POCKET CALENDAR OF SAINTS AND PEOPLE TO REMEMBER
by Brother Kenneth, CGA

A POCKET DICTIONARY OF THE CHRISTIAN CHURCH by Arthur L. Moore

A POCKET GUIDE FOR SERVERS
by Raymond Wilkinson

A POCKET GUIDE TO CHRISTIAN BELIEF
by Jean Smith

A POCKET GUIDE TO THE ANGLICAN CHURCH by Ronald H. Lloyd

A Pocket Guide to the Life and Meaning of Jesus

by

ARTHUR L. MOORE

Vicar of Hursley and Ampfield
and former Vice-Principal, Wycliffe Hall, Oxford

MOWBRAY
LONDON & OXFORD

ISBN 0 264 67011 6

First published 1986
by A. R. Mowbray & Co. Ltd,
Saint Thomas House, Becket Street,
Oxford, OX1 1SJ

Typeset by Comersgate Art Studios Ltd.
Printed in Great Britain by
Bocardo Press Limited, Oxford

British Library Cataloguing in Publication Data

Moore, Arthur L.
A pocket guide to the life and meaning of
Jesus.
1. Jesus Christ — Biography 2. Christian
biography — Palestine.
I. Title
232.9'01 BT301.2

CONTENTS

The first chapter of this book was first published 1983 in Mowbray's Enquirer's Library series of booklets.

Introduction

This little book tries to examine three matters: how Jesus lived, who he was, what he achieved.

The first part traces the course of his life as we can know it from the gospel records in the New Testament. The second part looks at the Christian claim that Jesus was both God and man and asks the two questions 'how' and 'why' – 'how can one person be at the same time human and divine?' and 'why did God, in Jesus, become man'. The final part concerns what theologians call the Atonement, the Christian affirmation that through his life, but especially by his death and resurrection, Jesus facilitated man's forgiveness, reconciled the world to God and established a whole new order of things.

Each of the three sections is self-contained and can be read, if desired, out of sequence.

1

The Life of Jesus

Who exactly was Jesus? When and where did he live? What was he like? How did he behave and why did he die? What was so special about him that long after his death millions still put their trust in him and look to him to give meaning to their lives?

THE EVIDENCE

Some time ago a few scholars decided that Jesus had never, in fact, existed! He was, they argued, simply an idea that certain religious people had expressed in story form. It is, however, entirely beyond doubt that a man named Jesus lived nearly 2,000 years ago in Palestine and was put to death under Pontius Pilate.

For one thing, certain secular historians testify to the fact. The Roman historian Tacitus (who died about AD 155) though not specially interested in Jesus or the Christian movement, wrote in his *Annals,* 'The name Christian comes from Christ who, during the principate of Tiberius, was put to death by the procurator Pontius Pilate'. Josephus, the Jewish historian, writing about AD 90 appears to know that Jesus was crucified by Pilate at the instigation of leading Jews.

For another thing, the New Testament itself is a witness that should not be disregarded, at least not if we are to behave as responsible enquirers. It is true that the New Testament writers were prejudiced; they believed Jesus to be a unique figure who accomplished in his life and by his death and resurrection a turning point in the world's history. It was because of this belief that they bothered to 'put pen to paper'. But such belief in no way invalidates their testimony – for all historians have points of view, presuppositions, attitudes towards the events they record. We have to ask whether the gospel writers acted responsibly or not; whether they were interested (or not) in recalling what actually happened. Many scholars conclude that considerable credence should be given to the gospel accounts and that, although there are minor differences between the various 'portraits' of Jesus, nevertheless in general they provide us with an honest and accurate account of the basic facts.

Here, only by way of illustration, are a few of the many reasons for their confidence:

1. Luke 1.3 shows that Luke at any rate thought that he was presenting a carefully researched and accurate account of Jesus' life and death.

2. The gospel writers retain some passages that they must have found difficult or perplexing (Mark 13.32 for instance), though it would have been a simple matter to omit them. Only considerations of honesty and of faithfulness to the tradition, presumably, led them to retain such passages in their accounts.

3. In 1 Corinthians 7, Paul carefully distinguishes

between his own teaching and what he calls a 'word of the Lord'. It is not entirely clear whether by this he means something Jesus had said during his earthly ministry or something said to Paul in a vision. But, either way, we see Paul taking pains to distinguish between his own (albeit wise) words and Jesus' words.

4. The earliest Christians lived in a world that had known Jesus and that remained, in general, hostile to him. Had the Christian community invented words and works of Jesus wholesale, there were not lacking those who could – and doubtless would – have responded, 'We were there and it did *not* happen like that', or, 'We heard him and he did *not* say that'.

If then we take the New Testament evidence seriously, what can we learn of this person Jesus?

THE BEGINNING

He was called 'Jesus of Nazareth' because he was brought up and plied his trade in that insignificant little town in the province of Galilee. But he was born in Bethlehem in the south, in the village from which the great king David 1,000 years before, had come; only a few miles from Jerusalem. We cannot say precisely *when* he was born. Certainly our calendar has misjudged things because Jesus' birth occurred whilst Herod the Great, who died in 4 BC was still alive! The most likely date seems to be about 7 BC.

According to Matthew and Luke, before Joseph and Mary were married Jesus was conceived through the action of the Holy Spirit upon Mary. Christians, therefore, speak of the virgin birth (meaning, strictly, the virgin conception). Since Paul makes no reference to this in his letters, the fact may well have been unknown to him and to the earliest Church and only became widely known in the later part of the first century. Mark's gospel and John's make no mention of the virgin birth, but both seem to know of rumours suggesting that Jesus was illegitimate (Mark 6.3, John 8.41, 9.29).

Closely associated with his birth, Luke mentions Jesus' circumcision, the purification of Mary and the offering of the child to the service of God – all three more or less rolled into one story (Luke 2.21–40). We are assured, at the outset, that the one of whom the gospels speak is not a divine being who only *seems* to be human, but one who is both truly divine and also truly human.

There is a veil over the whole period from Jesus' birth until the start of his public ministry, with one fascinating break given by Luke (2.41–52). According to this, Jesus was growing conscious of a special relation to God and of a special mission in life. 'In itself the story is a natural one, and does not include any supernatural features which might lead to sceptical estimates of its historicity. It portrays a growth in religious understanding such as might be expected in Jesus in view of his later life, and this understanding is complemented by his obedience to his parents' (I.H. Marshall, *The Gospel of Luke,* p.126).

Some time after our gospels were compiled, other writings (now called 'apocryphal gospels') delighted to fill in these 'hidden years' with fanciful accounts of Jesus' powers as a wonder-child. For instance: 'And when the Lord Jesus was seven years of age, he was on a certain day with other boys, his companions, about the same age. Who when they were at play, made clay into several shapes, namely asses, oxen, birds, and other figures, each boasting of his work, and endeavouring to exceed the rest. Then the Lord Jesus said to the boys, I will command these figures which I have made to walk. And immediately they moved, and when he commanded them to return, they returned. He had also made the figures of birds and sparrows which, when he commanded to fly, did fly, and when he commanded to stand still, did stand still . . . .' It is obvious that where our gospels (apart from Luke 2) have a sober, if tantalizing, silence such apocryphal stories have a fairytale quality and cannot supplement our knowledge of Jesus.

The first Christians were relatively uninterested in biographical details of this kind, just as they felt it was unimportant to record anything about Jesus' appearance (whether he was tall or short, slim or thick-set). They concentrated their interest, rather, on the words and works of the adult Jesus; as though to say to us, 'if you want to know who Jesus was, do not ask what he looked like nor how he grew in infancy, but rather attend to what he said and did in his public life – this will tell you what manner of man he was'.

GALILEE

Jesus was about thirty years old (Luke 3.23). Possibly encouraged by a religious revival initiated by John the

Baptist, he suddenly left home and began a public ministry in Galilee that lasted some three years (the 'synoptic' gospels, i.e. Matthew, Mark and Luke, do not specify more than a year, but John's gospel implies a longer period). It ended peacefully with Jesus' withdrawal from public attention in order to concentrate more exclusively on teaching his close group of followers. From his words and works in Galilee we learn much about Jesus' character and purpose.

1. *Fulfilment*

Matthew makes this a special theme of his story, but the earlier gospel of Mark also speaks of it: 'the time is fulfilled, the Kingdom of God is at hand' (Mark 1.15).

The ancient prophets of Israel had encouraged the hope that God would one day intervene in history to make his rule visible and put it beyond all doubt. They affirmed that God was *already* king; but his sovereignty was often called in question, especially by the prosperity of the wicked, the suffering of the righteous and the waywardness of nature. The hope, therefore, grew up that one day God would so act – by condemning the wicked, by blessing the righteous and by reordering nature – that his sovereign rule would no longer be questioned. He would raise up a new king (or priest, or both – the precise form of the expectation varied considerably) through whom this rule would be exercised. The thrust of Jesus' message was that this longed-for event was happening as he spoke. Luke makes the same point when he reports Jesus as saying, at the outset of his ministry, 'this day this scripture has been fulfilled in your hearing' (Luke 4.21).

Actually, Jesus fulfilled Israel's ancient hopes only in a very strange way. John the Baptist, who had challenged people to make ready for the awaited man of God, asked in bewilderment 'are you he who is to come, or shall we look for another?' (Matthew 11.3). And the religious leaders were very far from convinced that God was fulfilling, in Jesus, his promises of old! However, those who sided with him saw in Jesus the full expression and establishment of God's promised rule. The earliest disciples affirmed, in a kind of short creed, 'Jesus is Lord'; they meant that, in Jesus, God's sovereign will was fully expressed and fully obeyed. Paul similarly underlines the theme of fulfilment in Jesus when he writes of him, 'all the promises of God find their Yes in him' (2 Corinthians 1.20).

2. *Calling*

Jesus' first action in Galilee was to call individuals to follow him. They became his 'disciples', a word that simply means learners. Their calling was radical, spelling a thorough break with the past and with legitimate family and business ties. It was hazardous, involving sharing the uncertain lot of a wandering preacher; and it embraced self-sacrifice (see Mark 8.34).

Specifically twelve such followers were banded into an inner core, the nucleus of a new, reconstituted people of God. The number (more important than the precise identity of those who made up the group) recalls the tribes of Israel, for although the Church is never referred to in the New Testament as 'the new Israel' it is certainly *thought of* as such – Old Testament scriptures originally applying to Israel are applied to the New Testament Church (see e.g. 1 Peter 2.4–10).

The purpose of the group was twofold. First, to be with Jesus, to learn of him as an apprentice might learn the skills of his master. Secondly, to be sent out by Jesus, extending his own mission in the world. These two purposes found initial fulfilment during and immediately after Jesus' ministry but continue to find further fulfilment in the worshipping and witnessing life of the Church.

Just as Jesus was born into a modest home and was himself an artisan, so his followers too were, for the most part, drawn from the ordinary members of society. The twelve, typical of the Church throughout its history, were not exceptional men, specially talented or specially good. They were ordinary, knockabout people; many were cowards and at least one a traitor. What bound them together was Jesus himself whose call they could not ignore.

3. *Preaching*

The central theme of Jesus' proclamation was the presence of God's kingdom (or rule). His preaching was not, primarily, an appeal or exhortation, encouragement or challenge; it was simply the declaration of a truth – though not in a take-it-or-leave-it fashion, for he challenged people to acknowledge this truth and live in its light. Nevertheless it was affirmation rather than appeal. When Mark headed his story 'the beginning of the gospel of Jesus Christ' he emphasized this; for 'gospel' in the Old Testament signifies announcement of good news, especially news of victory.

In Matthew, Mark and Luke Jesus speaks of the kingdom; in John's gospel he speaks much more (and more directly) about himself. Here is a clue to the meaning of 'kingdom'. If we ask 'where is this kingdom?', the answer almost certainly is 'in Jesus himself'. (Origen, a second century theologian, commenting on Matthew 18.23, says 'as Jesus is the wisdom itself and the righteousness itself and the truth itself, so maybe he is also the kingdom itself . . . .') If we ask why, according to the synoptic gospels, Jesus preferred to speak of the kingdom rather than to say 'I am God's king', the answer is not immediately apparent; but we shall return to this theme of indirect self-disclosure later.

Jesus' favourite preaching technique was the parable. The Greek word *parabole* means, basically, an illustration. But the Hebrew background to the New Testament's use of this word provides a wider significance and means, besides illustration, an enigma or puzzle. When Jesus spoke his parables he was not offering easily understood anecdotes but puzzles!

4. *Teaching*

Jesus' practice was public proclamation (of a puzzling kind) followed by private elucidation to the inner group (Mark 4.33–34). His puzzles were not meant permanently to conceal but to challenge the hearer to struggle through to full understanding. Those who tried, and wanted to know, were given further teaching. (The fourth gospel presents the same idea in a different way; a long conversation during which understanding grows from partial to complete; see, for instance, John 9.)

So Jesus teaches his followers about prayer and discipleship, about private, domestic and social responsibilities. This is not simply good advice to all and sundry. It is teaching for those who see in Jesus their king and who believe themselves to be caught up in his rule. That is to say, Jesus' teaching relates primarily to those whose lives are touched by God's Spirit. When Jesus says (for example) 'Blessed are those who hunger and thirst for righteousness' (Matthew 5.6) he means 'happy the man moved by God's Spirit to long for the things of God'.

5. *Miracles*

One or two summary statements suggest that Jesus' ministry in Galilee was somewhat like a travelling dispensary (Mark 1.32–34)! John's gospel records fewer miracles but he selects highly dramatic ones.

What are we to make of these strange happenings? There is certainly no necessity to regard them as unhistorical, the inventions of a credulous early Church! If God was indeed present in Jesus, we might well expect that extraordinary things might happen. Everything depends on whether, as Paul puts it, 'God was in Christ reconciling the world to himself' (2 Corinthians 5.19). Our answer to this will determine our attitude to the miracles.

But what were micracles *for?* The obvious answer is that they expressed Jesus' care for needy people (see e.g. Mark 8.2). What, however, are we to make of the (apparently) many occasions when miracles did *not* happen? Was Jesus, on those occasions, lacking in compassion? Should we, perhaps, add that faith also was necessary, so that miracles were the response of love to faith? This ties in with Mark's statement about Jesus' failure in Nazareth ('because of their unbelief' Mark 6.5). However, in some cases people were healed without, apparently, having faith . . . .

Probably compassion was only a *partial* motivation of the miracles. To some extent they were simply an inevitable expression of the presence, in Jesus, of God's sovereign rule. They were signs of that presence (Matthew 12.28). But precisely because miracles were signs of the kingdom present in Jesus, they were to some extent an embarrassment to him. They tended to disclose too much, too clearly. Hence Jesus sometimes healed away from the crowds, sometimes commanded silence about it, sometimes used the recognized medical paraphernalia, so that the miraculous element would be minimized. Here again we confront the strange determination of Jesus to disclose the truth about himself in an indirect way.

6. *Conflict*

Here we meet one of the most puzzling aspects of the entire story. God, in Jesus, came to his own to fulfil his gracious promises; and he was rejected out of hand (John

1.11)! Already, when he entered the world as a helpless baby, there was found not much room for him. And, though in Galilee Jesus went about doing good, immediately there were those who grumbled at him; and it was not long before a definite decision was taken to do away with him (Mark 3.6).

The reason for this, on one level, was because Jesus startled people. He appeared to claim that he was God's special envoy, yet he was clearly a mere carpenter. He sat light to cherished religious customs and the ritual demands of the law. He seemed to pose a threat to the *status quo* and so to the privileged position of the powerful. At a deeper level, maybe, we have to say that it somehow belongs to man to bite the hand that feeds him! In rejecting Jesus men were doing what they are always doing; turning from light and life . . . .

So the Galilean ministry was a mixture of many things. And though there was that undercurrent of antagonism, it might be reckoned a time of relative popularity and success. What was the point of it all? Essentially, Jesus' purpose was to present himself to the world as:

God's chosen or anointed one.

Jesus never spoke of himself as 'Christ' (meaning anointed), but when others used it of him he did not reject it. In John's gospel Jesus speaks of himself not infrequently as God's Son, one who enjoys special affinity with God and owes God special obedience. Generally, Jesus referred to himself as 'Son of Man'. This is a strangely comprehensive term, because on the one hand it could mean 'one who shares all the characteristics of mortal man', whilst on the other hand (thinking of its use in Daniel 7) it could mean 'one who shares the characteristics of a divine ruler', a being from heaven with authority and power. It was therefore an extremely ambiguous term, yet one containing claims of the highest order.

The man of service

Mark 10.45 says, 'the Son of Man came not to be served but to serve'. In representing God to men and in presenting himself to the world as God's chosen instrument, Jesus did not lord it over man as though it belonged to divine sovereignty to manipulate and to bully. Rather, God showed himself to be humble, seeking the well-being of others rather than of himself, caring for all and sundry, but especially for those who were socially outcast, physically or spiritually oppressed.

The man of faith

Jesus said, 'if you have faith as a grain of mustard seed, you will say to this mountain, "Move hence to yonder place", and it will move; and nothing will be impossible to you' (Matthew 17.20) – and so Jesus lived! He was himself the man of faith who lived out of the hand of his Father, looking to him to achieve his purposes through the Son, trusting him to attend to all his needs, calling down from God whatever was necessary to effect his will and to meet the needs of men.

We must now return to an oddity we have already

noted. Jesus generally presented himself to his contemporaries in an indirect way. Why was this? Could he not simply have said, 'I am God's anointed', or, 'I have come to establish God's rule'? The answer is that an indirect self-presentation was appropriate, for two reasons.

(i) It would hardly have become one of a humble disposition to make (however legitimately) large claims for himself. That is why at the outset Jesus submitted to a baptism that, strictly speaking, he might have refused. He took his place humbly alongside all other men.

(ii) It belongs to God's purposes that men should have the opportunity to come to a personal, voluntary and growing realization of the truth, rather than to have truth forced upon them. Clearly if God were to present himself to men in direct fashion, men would bow down and worship whether they really wished to or not! So God reveals himself with a degree of hiddenness; some light is given, but not too much.

The story of Moses (in Exodus 33.17–23) is instructive. Moses asks to see what God is really like. But Moses cannot see the undiluted glory of God and retain his senses. So God shows him a little. The story of the Transfiguration is also instructive. Jesus' real splendour is for a moment revealed, and Peter makes his crazy suggestion (Mark 9.5) because he is practically out of his mind! There was too much light.

In order that men might come to faith there must be disclosure – so Jesus spoke God's words and worked God's works; but there must also be concealment – so Jesus spoke in riddles and worked miracles in relative ambiguity. He was God with us (revelation) in the form of a servant (concealment).

STRATEGIC WITHDRAWAL

The work in Galilee ended with Peter's acknowledgement of Jesus as Christ. At that point, Jesus withdrew to the north and wandered apparently aimlessly about. Some have seen in this an expression of Jesus' frustration (at the crowd's superficial response) or his disappointment (at God's failure to intervene dramatically). However, the obvious purpose is stated in Mark 9.30–31; the need to teach the disciples further.

In particular Jesus needed to speak to them of his impending death. There were enough instances in Israel's history of God's messengers being rejected and killed for the disciples to anticipate trouble. Nevertheless, the suggestion that God's anointed, the new Davidic king, might have to die was quite unthinkable to them (see Mark 8.32). Despite his efforts, Jesus' death still caught the twelve unawares so that they all abandoned him and returned to their former business. However, during this period of withdrawal the foundation was laid on which, later, Jesus could build a proper understanding of what his death had accomplished.

During this time the Transfiguration occurred, a strange event with some similarities to Jesus' baptism. The story reminds us that though this man of God is shortly to be rejected by men, he has divine approval. It points also to the future when the hiddenness of Jesus' glory will be over and when God's truth will be seen without the slightest ambiguity or contradiction. What Christians have since learned to call the Parousia of Jesus, i.e. his final coming in splendour, is seen in the Transfiguration in an anticipatory way and the promise of his final return is confirmed.

JERUSALEM

The northern wanderings over, Jesus moves southwards, still teaching the twelve but drawing ever closer to the capital where he faced certain hostility and death.

He entered Jerusalem in style (Mark 11.1–10)! Actually, since no immediate action was taken by the ever-vigilant Romans and since the incident was not mentioned at the trial, it was probably a quite ordinary affair. Only in retrospect was it seen that Jesus had fulfilled the promise of Zechariah 9.9 and come as the lowly, peace-making king.

His first act was to 'cleanse' the temple. The place was meant to symbolize God's presence and to foster worship. In practice there had grown up around the cycle of sacrificial worship something of a racket in the sale of animals and in currency exchange. And this business was conducted not simply nearby but actually in the temple area, in the part set aside for Gentiles. Jesus' indignant action was a plea for genuine religion.

Jesus speaks of the future (Mark 13 and similarly Matthew 24, Luke 21). His prediction about the destruction of the temple (Mark 13.2) brings to mind the expectation that one day God would establish a quite new temple, and a new Jerusalem; indeed, a whole new world. So we are given a general description of this cataclysmic event (Mark 13.24–27). This divine act will not be unheralded; a whole range of situations, especially domestic and political disturbances, would point to that future event and be reminders that one day conflict would cease. So we are given a description of such 'signs' of the End (Mark 13.5–23).

Of course, what we long to know is 'when'! This chapter gives two directives. First, the *signs* are happening all the time; even Jesus' contemporaries (not to mention successive generations) experience them (Mark 13.28–31). Secondly, the *End* itself cannot be dated, for God keeps this information to himself (Mark 13.32–37). The discourse, strange to modern ears, is a reminder that contemporary events are eloquent of the future and the wise will allow the present scene to point beyond itself to the ultimate purposes of God for his world.

At this point, the story becomes quite detailed and carefully put together (contrast the general introductions to events in Galilee such as 'and then' or 'and it happened'). Indeed, one scholar some years ago declared our gospels to be 'passion narratives with extended introductions' and, in a sense, they are. Almost certainly the story of Jesus' final days in Jerusalem was compiled and circulated at an earlier stage than the story of his Galilean ministry.

Jesus shared a final meal with his friends. It was Passover time (the synoptic gospels say the evening *of;*

John says the evening *before* Passover). Passover was a memorial meal celebrating the event when God's people escaped slavery in Egypt. It spoke of the pilgrimage of the people of God, moving out of bondage into the place of liberty where God could be worshipped without fear or hindrance.

Into this meal, already loaded with spiritual value and meaning, Jesus injected further significance. He took bread and said that it spoke of his body; wine, and affirmed that it pointed to his blood. A new kind of remembrance meal was inaugurated and a new liberation celebrated; a new covenant (we think of Jeremiah 31.31) was established, new fellowship with the visiting, liberating God facilitated. The meal was from the start a central aspect of Christian worship (Acts 2.46) and continues, in most churches, to be so.

Judas, 'one of the twelve', was unmasked at this meal; yet not without the right hand of fellowship being extended to the end. This celebration meal is not for the select few alone but for the whole motley collection of needy people whose release from captivity Jesus effected.

Jesus' trial divides into two; that before the Sanhedrin (central council of the Jews) and that before Pilate (local Roman governor).

Judas had facilitated the arrest. He led the authorities to the secluded spot to which Jesus resorted each evening and here he was taken without a commotion (see Mark 14.2). It was night and, so far as we know, night-time meetings of the Sanhedrin were illegal; so the assembly described in Mark 14.53 was probably an informal gathering to decide action and to formulate a charge. At daybreak the informal decision was ratified and Jesus was sent up to Pilate with a charge alleging that he was a political agitator and a threat to peace.

Pilate made some effort to achieve Jesus' release. But Rome tended to post to Palestine weak officials, and Pilate was certainly no match for the wily Jewish leaders who were determined to have Jesus condemned. Even his suggestion that he release a prisoner at this festal time (a kind of limited amnesty) backfired and a genuine terrorist was freed.

Jesus made no attempt to defend himself and he was condemned and summarily executed. He accepted that, though what was being done could not be excused, nevertheless his suffering and death were all part of the Father's purpose for him – and, through him, for the world (John 12.32). That does not mean that he found the experience easy. From the description of his prayer in Gethsemane and his cry on the cross ('My God, my God, why has thou forsaken me?') it is clear that the pain of those final hours defies human description or appreciation.

We shall consider shortly what all this means: how, precisely, Jesus' death came about and what, exactly, it achieved. For the moment, notice one important element in the Jerusalem ministry which might easily be overlooked, the element of faith.

In Galilee we saw a man of faith who by prayer drew

down from heaven resources for a needy world. The man of faith called upon God and found answer. But there is another aspect to faith.

In the Book of Job 'Satan' asked God, 'Does Job serve God for nothing?' Men do not turn from God if indeed God is a kind of panacea for all ills. But neither do men relate to such a God in sheer trust, for his sake alone; they relate to him for what they can get out of him. In Jerusalem and on Calvary Jesus is asked 'Will you serve God for nothing?', 'Will you trust God even when he seems not to hear you?'.

Already at the outset Jesus had experienced the pressure of the so-called Temptations. He resisted them. But the real test came at the end. God, who had generously given all things into his Son's hands, now allows him systematically to be deprived of it all – family, friends, justice, dignity, nourishment, life itself; and, hanging on the cross with the judgement of Deuteronomy 21.23 in mind, he was deprived even of hope. Will he *now* trust God? Will the man of faith repose confidence in God when God seems no longer to warrant it? The answer is 'yes' for he endured to the end – hence the cry of triumph, 'It is finished' (John 19.30).

In the light of this perhaps we should speak of two kinds of faith, or two aspects of faith:

1. 'Galilee faith' which refuses to take 'no' for an answer, which requires God to be faithful to his promise and give when we ask, open when we knock.

2. 'Jerusalem faith' which allows God to say 'no' if he chooses, which adds 'nevertheless your will not mine' to

prayer – not as a kind of 'let out' in case what we ask is not forthcoming, but as a serious acknowledgement that in our relationship with him, God is the senior partner. 'Galilee faith' is exhilerating and triumphant, but it is 'Jerusalem faith' that 'brings the gift that angels cannot bring, a heart that trusts even in the dark'.

Three times Jesus had spoken of his impending death; each time he had added that he would rise again. And that is what happened.

Mark's gospel records no resurrection appearances (the gospel ended, in its original form, at 16.8) but we are assured that Christ was alive. Matthew speaks of resurrection appearances in Galilee, Luke of appearances in Jerusalem, and John's gospel speaks of appearances in both places. Paul mentions some of these and adds others (1 Corinthians 15.4–8). It is clear that there is some untidiness about the details. Some people find in this evidence of secondariness. But others take the view that an event of this extraordinary (indeed unique) kind is likely to be reported with a certain confusion.

ALIVE FOR EVER

The New Testament gives us no actual proof that Jesus rose from the dead. Instead, we are given three encouragements:

1. The empty tomb. What happened to the body of Jesus? D.H. Lawrence wrote a poignant short story based on the idea that Jesus was not quite dead when he was buried: that he subsequently revived sufficiently to

emerge from the tomb and meet with his followers. Only later did he actually die. For such a reconstruction the New Testament offers no slightest support! Nor, indeed, for the suggestion that the disciples secretly stole the body and disposed of it elsewhere. Nor, again, does the New Testament support the rather bizarre idea that the first visitors simply went to the wrong grave and were re-directed ('he is not here: see the place where they laid him', Mark 16:6!). The brute facts of the empty tomb, of the inability of hostile contemporaries to produce Jesus' body, and of the lack of any convincing theory supported by what evidence we have to explain the empty tomb, remain strong encouragements to accept the truth that Jesus rose from the dead.

2. The resurrection appearances. Of course, there are various ways of accounting for these. We might conjecture that the disciples were hallucinating, for though group hallucination is seldom encountered the phenomenon is not unknown. Or we might argue, as many modern scholars do, that in describing such appearances the disciples were not wishing to be understood literally but were proclaiming in pictorial form the deeper truth that Jesus' death was not a tragedy but a strange victory: that he was vanquished by men but vindicated by God. However, there is no suggestion in the New Testament evidence that when the disciples said 'Jesus died' they meant us to understand them literally but when they said 'Jesus was raised from the dead' they meant us to understand them metaphorically. The resurrection

appearances may remain for us, as they seem to have been for the first disciples, convincing support for the fact of Jesus' resurrection.

3. The rise of the Christian church. If Jesus did not rise from the dead 'we are of all men most miserable' says St. Paul (1 Corinthians 15.19) – for unless God raised him up Jesus' death was indeed a tragic waste and a shocking injustice. But St. Paul and his fellow Christians were patently not 'of all men most miserable'! With extraordinary zeal and courage and with an astonishing sense of conviction they proclaimed Jesus and the resurrection, endured insults, shame, punishment and even death, won over adherents throughout the then known world and set in motion a movement which flourishes to this day. Of course, in the history of mankind people have been known to suffer and die on behalf of a lie: the intensity with which a conviction is held does not guarantee the rightness of that conviction. Nevertheless the rise and continuance of the church is a strong support for the belief that though he 'was crucified, dead and buried' yet 'on the third day he rose again from the dead'.

What does it mean? Simply that the cross achieved what it set out to achieve; that God was pleased with the obedience of the man of faith, his own anointed who trusted to the end; that God accepted the sacrifice and through it effected the liberation and renewal of his people. It means also that Jesus is alive into all eternity, death no longer having any hold over him. Christians worship not a dead Jesus but a living Lord; one who is alive not by virtue of having escaped death, but by virtue of having experienced it in all its anguish, yet coming out on the other side.

The resurrection gives meaning to the cross. But the resurrection is not 'merely' meaning, a thought in picture form. It is meaning *through* event. The New Testament invites us to accept that Jesus was just as really taken up out of the tomb as beforehand he was really hoisted onto a cross and lowered into a grave.

DOES IT MATTER?

Such, roughly speaking (and with many scholarly arguments ignored or side-stepped) is what we can know about Jesus. Does it matter?

It matters if we are concerned with traditional Christianity. Christianity is not a set of ideas about God; not a world-view; not a code of behaviour – though it involves these things. Christianity is a statement about events in which 'God visited and redeemed his people' (Luke 1.68). If (within rough limits) Jesus did not do and say what our gospels maintain that he did and said, we might continue to be Christian in some sense, but not Christian in the traditional sense.

It matters if we are concerned with the 'truth as it is in Jesus'. Truth, according to the New Testament, is not simply a set of correct propositions but a person, Jesus (John 14.6). Knowing a person involves the heart and the will; but it involves also, and perhaps first and foremost, the mind. So 'knowing Jesus' begins with 'knowing about him', weighing up the evidence and paying heed to what the gospels tell us about him.

It matters if we are concerned to worship the true Lord of the Church. For who is this Lord? To whom are hymns sung and prayers said? The answer is that the Church's present and living Lord is the Jesus of whom the gospels speak, the one who lived, died and rose again; Jesus who is the same yesterday, today and for ever (Hebrews 13.8). It is 'This same Jesus', the Jesus of history who is also now the Church's Lord and the Church's hope.

2

Jesus, God and Man

According to the wording of the 'Nicene creed' (a formula of faith agreed in the fourth century) Christians believe in 'one Lord Jesus Christ, the only-begotten Son of God . . . who for us men and for our salvation came down from heaven . . . and was made man'. Utterly unique, this Jesus is at the same time truly God and yet equally truly man. But this assertion of faith gives rise to two fundamental questions: '*How* can one person be at the same time divine and human?' and '*why* did God become man?' The first question is concerned with the nature of Jesus and the second with his function or work.

THE EVIDENCE

1. *Really a man*

The New Testament writers are in no doubt that Jesus was really human. Matthew and Luke relate infancy stories telling how Jesus came into the world as a baby born of his mother Mary. To be sure, the conception of this baby was unique, for in the place of a human father we hear of the activity of the Spirit of God. But, once conceived, the baby grew and was born in the usual manner. Indeed, the New Testament stresses the ordinariness of the occasion (though, at the same time, it relates strange portents that heralded and accompanied it). Luke tells us that the child 'increased in wisdom and stature, and in favour with God and man' (Luke 2.52) which is as much as to say 'he grew into a fine upstanding lad'. Luke also relates an incident (Luke 2.41–51) which shows Jesus to have been a somewhat precocious youngster, yet one who generally did as his parents told him. As an adult Jesus lived with brothers and sisters in a very ordinary home, plied his trade as a carpenter and was subject to all the rough and tumble of family and social life.

During his ministry Jesus exercised remarkable powers: power to heal sick people; power to manipulate material and, for isntance, change water into wine; power even to make dead people come back to life. And yet the New Testament writers do not hesitate to tell us that this same Jesus knew hunger (Matthew 21.18) and thirst (John 4.7), that he was tired out from a long journey (John 4.6), that he was deeply moved at the death of a friend (John 11.35), that he was capable of anger (Mark 3.5) and that he was troubled beyond words at his own impending death (Mark 14.34, Luke 22.44). Like any mortal man, his life ran its course, came to its end and led inevitably to the grave.

At the same time, the New Testament writers affirm that Jesus' humanity was different from ours. He was really human; yet he was without sin! Jesus himself alludes to this sinlessness (John 8.46); the writer of the letter to the Hebrews makes it the cornerstone of his thesis about Jesus as our high priest (Hebrews 4.15, 7.26f, 9.14 and 10.12) and Peter states quite bluntly that Jesus 'committed no sin' (1 Peter 2.22).

2. *Truly God*

There was something unique about Jesus. It was not simply that he was a special person, not even extra-special (without sin). The New Testament insists that he was truly divine.

His conception by God's own life-giving Spirit points in this direction. His sense of filial relationship to God (Mark 1.11) disclosed itself in his customary address to God as 'my Father' (using an intimate family form of address). It was this conviction of sharing in God's own divine being that so outraged his opponents (John 10.33). He exercised the divine right to forgive sins almost as a matter of course (Mark 2.5–6). And although the ancient world reckoned with wonder-workers with extraordinary powers, the New Testament writers clearly believed that Jesus' miracles were signs not simply that he was a prophet or magician but that he embodied God's own sovereign rule (see Matthew 12.28). Matthew records the angel's words to Joseph that Jesus should be called 'Emmanuel, which means, God with us' (Matthew 1.23).

Some of the passages in the New Testament which contain very early summaries of Christian faith (what we might call our earliest creeds) speak of Jesus in the highest possible terms (see Philippians 2.6–11, Colossians 1.15–20, 1 Timothy 3.16, Hebrews 1.3 and 1 Peter

3.18–20). But perhaps the most unequivocal statement of Jesus' divinity is found in the opening verse of John's gospel where we are told that the 'Word' (clearly to be identified with Jesus) was not only *with* God but that '*the Word was God*' (John 1.1).

If outright statements of Jesus' divinity are rare in the New Testament this is probably because the earliest Christians, with their Jewish background, held firmly to a belief in *one* God (mono-theism: unlike non-Jews who believed in 'lords many and gods many', 1 Corinthians 8.5), and were anxious to avoid any suggestion that they worshipped two Gods. Such, however, was the impression he made upon them that, despite this risk, they could do no other than affirm that somehow Jesus was divine.

Here, then, in outline is the evidence. It is most succinctly expressed in verses from John's gospel: 'In the beginning was the Word . . . and the Word became flesh and dwelt among us' (John 1.1 and 1.14). Similarly, writing to the Colossians, Paul says that in Jesus 'all the fullness of God was pleased to dwell' and goes on immediately to speak of Jesus' death 'in his body of flesh' (Colossians 1.19 and 1.22). Jesus' divinity and humanity are sharply juxtaposed. The New Testament presents the evidence but it does not elucidate it. We are told *that* Jesus was both God and man, but we are not told *how* this could be. We are left in no doubt that God's purpose in it all was not flippant but utterly serious; yet we are not told in detail or at length what that purpose was.

Perhaps the New Testament writers were still too vividly aware of Jesus as a person to be able objectively to reflect on the data. Perhaps (as seems more likely) they were simply so taken up with their immediate work of proclaiming him to their contemporaries that they just had to leave to later generations the task of pressing questions and reaching towards fuller understanding.

THE STRUGGLE TO UNDERSTAND

Once the Church turned to the task, the problems associated with the Incarnation (i.e. the event in which God became man) occupied its attention for some time. Various interpretations were explored, various suggestions debated; councils were held and certain definitions more or less agreed. Much of the debate sounds to us remote. Here, for instance, is an extract from the so-called Athanasian creed (to be found in the Prayer Book immediately before the Litany): 'for the right faith is, that we believe and confess: that our Lord Jesus Christ, the Son of God, is God and Man: God, of the Substance of the Father, begotten before the worlds: and Man, of the Substance of his Mother, born in the world; Perfect God, and perfect Man: of a reasonable soul and human flesh subsisting; Equal to the Father, as touching his Godhead: and inferior to the Father, as touching his Manhood. Who, although he be God and Man: yet he is not two, but one Christ; One: not by conversion of the Godhead into flesh: but by taking of the Manhood into God; One altogether; not by confusion of Substance: but by unity of Person. For as the reasonable soul and flesh is one man: so God and Man is one Christ. . .'.

This may indeed strike us as rather quaint. But the questions to which the author addressed himself were, and are, real and important.

TWO APPROACHES

To cut a long story short and grossly to over-simplify we may say that in the days of the early Church there were two kinds of cultural or religious heritage, two kinds of intellectual approach to things. We may call them Hebrew and Greek, and we may not unfairly summarize them as follows:

1. The 'Hebrew' approach tended to be pragmatic. It concentrated on the known facts, probing them to discover underlying meaning. History – the ongoing sequence of events – was regarded as very important as was also the world of nature: matter mattered, because although fallen, God had made the world and would some day redeem it. Moreover, God made himself known through events and things, whether an Exodus or a burning bush, a meal or a tent of meeting.

This pragmatic, 'Hebrew' approach or disposition of mind naturally began any investigation of the Incarnation from the humanity of Jesus. It began with the blunt fact of Jesus of Nazareth, the carpenter, the real man. This approach started at ground level and worked upwards, with the result that Jesus' divinity was, so to speak, fitted in to his humanity.

2. The 'Greek' approach concentrated on the world of

ideas, the inner meaning of things and the speculative world of thought. This 'idealist' approach tended to minimize the significance of history ('just one darned thing after another') and to look for meaning *apart* from events rather than *in* events. Similarly this approach tended to regard the material world less than seriously and it reckoned the spiritual more signifcant than the material (and the two as quite distinct).

Grappling with the Incarnation, this 'Greek' approach naturally began from the divinity of Jesus, his unseen spiritual reality. It then worked its way downwards to Jesus' humanity. The result was that Jesus' humanity was, so to speak, fitted in to his divinity.

Let it be said again, this description is a gross over-simplification. Yet, like most caricatures, it is not altogether unfair.

TWO ERRORS

1. If you follow what we are calling a Greek disposition, then you will certainly do justice to Jesus' divinity but you may fail to do justice to his real humanity. It is, of course, perfectly acceptable to begin an investigation by concentrating on Jesus' divinity – after all, you must begin somewhere. But the danger is that you may understand the Incarnation in such a way that Jesus remains truly God but is not really man. In this way, justice would not be done to the New Testament evidence (which, as we have seen, points to the real humanity as well as to the divinity of Jesus). This is an error into which

many fell in the early years of the Church's life. Some indeed already in New Testament days had made this mistake (almost certainly the first epistle of John, for instance, is intended to oppose such a view: see especially 1 John 4.2–3).

A Greek approach falls easily into this error. It is called 'docetism' from a Greek word meaning 'to seem', for opponents rightly object that the view whilst affirming that Jesus was truly God suggests that he only *seemed* to be a man.

2. If, on the other hand, you follow what we are calling a Hebrew disposition, then you will certainly evaluate Jesus' humanity highly, but you may fail to do full justice to his divinity. It is perfectly acceptable to begin the investigation by concentrating on Jesus' humanity – as before, you have to begin somewhere. But the danger is that Jesus will be regarded as fully human but somewhat less than truly divine. It may be suggested that he was 'adopted' into the Godhead as a kind of reward for, or consequence of, a truly inspired life. But an elevated man remains, in the last analysis, less than truly God.

This error, known as Ebionite (from a Hebrew word meaning 'poor men'), flourished within mainly Jewish-Christian circles and existed for some centuries, mainly in the East.

'No-through road'

Christians thought hard and long about the Incarnation, and what eventually emerged after considerable debate was not so much a full clarification (of what we mean when we say Jesus was God and man) as rather sign-posts delineating the boundaries within which correct understanding should be sought. In particular, the view that Jesus was truly God but only seemed to be a man, and the view that Jesus was really human but somewhat less than divine, were both classified as errors – heresy.

The decision was taken at a celebrated council of church leaders held at Chalcedon (a town in Asia Minor, nearly opposite Byzantium) in AD 451. Over five hundred bishops attended. A great deal of controversy preceded it, much of it acrimonious, for feelings ran high and the issues at stake were regarded as crucial. After days of fierce debate the council ruled that both the 'docetic' and 'Ebionite' views were wrong. It decreed that Jesus was 'consubstantial with the Father as touching his Godhead, and consubstantial with us as touching his Manhood'; that is to say, he was truly God and truly man (in the language of the Council *vere deus et vere homo*).

TWO FURTHER ERRORS

It is not enough simply to say that Jesus is both human and divine. This, indeed, must be affirmed. But we must press further and ask 'How can one man be at the same time both human and divine?', 'How can two so disparate beings co-exist in the same one person?'.

1. *A Mixture of two*

One line of thought that appealed to some was this: Jesus

was both human and divine as a result of a kind of fusion of the two. Jesus was, on this view, a kind of amalgam: so much percentage human, so much divine.

The chief name associated with this view is a certain Eutyches who was head of a large monastery at Constantinople in the first half of the fifth century. Eutyches was clearly troubled by the suggestion of some that Jesus might be described as a kind of schizoid, a person with two personalities, two wills, two centres of consciousness. Such a suggestion seemed to him monstrous and he preferred to lean in the opposite direction, maintaining that Jesus had only one 'nature', a mixture of God and man. (His view is called 'monophysite' from the Greek words meaning 'one' and 'nature'.)

To some extent this sounds so reasonable that we may wonder why the same Council of Chalcedon labelled it an error. But opponents of the view rightly protested that a mixture of human and divine would produce someone *half*-human and *half*-divine, *not* someone wholly and altogether both. Justice, they argued, would be done neither to Jesus' real humanity nor to his full divinity. They were surely right. We cannot claim that the child of an English father and an Indian mother is altogether English and altogether Indian: rather, he is a new blend sharing some of the characteristics (but not all) of the father and some (but again not all) of the mother. Whereas of Jesus (so the early Christians maintained) we need to say that he is wholly divine and wholly human. Eutyches failed in this.

2. *A Monster of two*

Another possibility appealed to some, namely that Jesus had two distinct 'natures', one human and the other divine (the debate was not helped by having to make use of terms drawn from philosophy or science or some other discipline and not altogether designed for the theological purpose which they were pressed into serving; furthermore, some were – and still are – ambiguous and some carried overtones which were quite unhelpful).

The main character associated with this view was one Nestorius who died about the middle of the fifth century. For a time he was Bishop of Constantinople, but his opponents succeeded in having him banished to Upper Egypt where he ended his days. Nestorius wanted to do full justice to Jesus' true humanity and true divinity. He saw clearly how unsatisfactory was the suggestion of Eutyches who presented us with a Jesus neither truly man nor truly God. So Nestorius affirmed that the divine and the human in Jesus were entirely distinct and that Jesus had two centres of consciousness, two wills and was, in fact, two 'persons' – though, to do Nestorius justice, he maintained that these two were entirely in harmony with each other.

As before, we can see the reasonableness of the suggestion. But again, it will not do. Nestorius presents us with a monster. Two people inhabiting the same frame is hardly less grotesque than one person with two heads! And we can hardly claim that the one child of mixed parents is, in reality, two children! Nestorius certainly meant well (so, of course, did Eutyches) but his suggestion does not really help us in explaining *how* Jesus was truly God and also truly man.

Once again, the Council of Chalcedon set up a 'no-through road' sign. In opposition to Eutyches the Council decreed that Jesus had two 'natures – without confusion, without change, without division, without separation'. And against Nestorius it maintained that these two 'natures' existed within one (not two) 'persons', one single being and not a kind of schizoid.

THE STRUGGLE CONTINUES

The Council of Chalcedon set up boundaries. It did not solve problems. The New Testament data about Jesus remains and attempts to understand the 'how' and the 'why' continue.

1. *Human really means divine*

In the nineteenth century a serious attempt was made to resolve the tension between the two 'natures' in Jesus by suggesting that divine and human are not really categories far removed from one another but that humanity at its best is, more or less, divine.

This suggestion owed much to the mood of evolutionary optimism that prevailed at the time colouring most scientific, philosophical and theological thought. Such a mood was, perhaps, understandable because scientific discoveries and technical advances (in medicine, in communications, in methods of production, etc.) made it look rather as though man was, indeed, maturing towards a new perfection in which he might be regarded as little less than god!

The conclusion of such thought is that the great gulf fixed – as ancient Hebrews supposed – between God and man is daily growing smaller. Jesus, we might say, was ahead of his age. He was man at his best, man as we all shall shortly become: and, as such, he was divine.

We seem to have here a neat solution of the ancient puzzle about Jesus' humanity and divinity. But it suffers from two drawbacks. First, the underlying thesis is wrong. Few people experiencing the massive traumas of twentieth century life could suppose that 'every day in every way we are getting better and better'. We are doubtless more ready than were our grandfathers to assent to Isaiah's insight that God's ways and thoughts are higher, far higher than ours (Isaiah 55.9).

Secondly, this suggestion is, in fact, not a resolution of the tension but an evasion of it. It no longer affirms the divine and human in Jesus but only the one 'divine-equals-human' element. This is little other than the old 'monophysite' teaching advocated by Eutyches and, as we have seen, ruled out by the Council of Chalcedon. We need an understanding of Jesus that does justice to the real difference between God and man, not one that simply identifies the two.

2. *Not altogether divine*

A different attempt to probe the mystery of Jesus was made by a group of English theologians at the turn of the century, taking as their key Paul's statement (possibly quoting an earlier 'hymn') in Philippians 2.7 to the effect that Jesus, the pre-existent Son of God, equal with God in every way, 'emptied' himself in becoming man. They suggested that Jesus shed some aspect of his divine nature and in this way divine and human were able to co-exist in him. (It is known as the 'kenotic' theory from the Greek word meaning 'empty'.)

Like so many others, this view sounds promising but it suffers from serious flaws. First, it is not clear what the 'emptying' mentioned in Philippians 2.7 means. Perhaps Wesley was right when he wrote in his well-known hymn 'And it can be. . .' that Jesus 'emptied himself of all but love. . .'. Since, however, God *is* love (1 John 4.8), if Jesus discarded everything except love, he discarded nothing essential to the divine nature; he only put off some inessential, as a man might take off his overcoat. But to suppose that some peripheral aspects whether of humanity or divinity were absent in Jesus helps little in understanding how Jesus can be really (in essentials) God and man.

Of course, secondly, the scholars of whom we are thinking maintained that Jesus had discarded not merely something peripheral but something basic to divinity. In this case, however, we are quickly back to the old (Ebionite) view that Jesus was truly man but somewhat less than really divine (the view ruled out by the New Testament evidence and by the Council of Chalcedon!).

1. *Not divine at all*

A number of contemporary scholars (whose views are, to

some extent, represented in the *Myth of God Incarnate*, edited by John Hick) also follow a path which leads in the same direction.

We must begin, they say, with the humanity of Jesus and we must ask 'What was special about the man Jesus that caused his followers to speak of him in language normally reserved for God?'. They, Jesus' first disciples, used such language about Jesus because (so the scholars argue) that was the kind of language available and that was the kind of thought-world in which they lived. Once we have discovered what was special about the man Jesus, we shall be able to express ourselves without recourse to such language and thought-patterns, because other language and other ideas are available to us: we might speak of him as 'fully personal' or say that 'he lived an authentic existence'.

This approach rejects the 'no-through road' sign set up by Chalcedon. It resolves the problem about the Incarnation by simply concluding that Jesus was only a man, albeit a very special (and, if you like, a unique) man. However, it is not at all clear that when the New Testament writers used of Jesus the language appropriate to God they meant something quite different. It is far from proven that when the first Christians wanted to describe someone who made a special impact on them, they had no alternative but to use 'divine' terms; in fact they had a variety of words and ideas available to them ('angel' is an obvious example that springs to mind).

4. *Not really human*

A suggestion put forward mainly by Catholic theologians runs as follows: in order that the divine and human might co-exist in Jesus, the humanity which he took was changed; it was no longer fallen but perfected humanity. This perfect manhood that Jesus assumed was no longer incompatible with true divinity.

Clearly this suggestion has merit. The New Testament (as we have noted) certainly affirms that Jesus was sinless. This already means that his humanity was not entirely the same as ours. Indeed, it means that it was different in a rather significant respect. For, as I grow, I find myself already at odds within myself, at odds with others about me, if I ponder on it, at odds with God. To be human means to be this kind of a person, a sinner from cradle to grave. It means to be subject to the frustrations and limitations of an errant will, of a deficient conscience, an inadequate wisdom and a rebellious nature. If Jesus did not share humanity *of this sort,* then he did not share *our* humanity.

Nevertheless, this view cannot be regarded as altogether satisfactory. The New Testament does not explain, but it does affirm that although Jesus was 'without sin' he nonetheless shared solidarity with us in our humanity. He took to himself a humanity which was decidedly ours, however different from us he managed to be. The letter to the Hebrews (4.15) is obviously struggling to do justice both to his solidarity with us, and to his difference from us, when it says of Jesus'we have not a high priest who is unable to sympathise with our weaknesses, but one who in every respect has been tempted as we are' (the solidarity) 'yet without sin' (the difference). If we too narrowly insist on the difference and posit for Jesus a humanity altogether different from ours, we slip into that most ancient of errors (docetism) in which Jesus is regarded as truly divine but as not really (only seemingly) human. According to Chalcedon (not to mention the New Testament) this will not do.

This, in merest outline, is something of the story of the struggle that has gone on, and that continues, in seeking to understand what the New Testament means when it points us to Jesus' real humanity and to his real divinity. And we must frankly admit that though we necessarily strive after deeper understanding, we continue to be baffled. In many ways we find ourselves treading the same old paths and coming up against the same dead-ends. Much of our thinking has to be negative: we state what we intend to deny and what we know is unacceptable. Beyond this, progress is indeed slow.

But so far we have been pondering only the first of the questions posed by the New Testament evidence, the first question concerning the Incarnation, namely 'how' can one person be both God and man. It is time we turned to the other question, 'why'.

WHY DID GOD BECOME MAN?

Here we shall simply look at some of the clues offered us by the New Testament:

1. *Not for the fun of it!*

Straightaway we must notice that the Bible gives no support to the view, seriously held from time to time, that God became man in order to enlarge his own experience. There is not the least hint that God was bored and decided to set out on an adventure! Nor that he was curious to know what it might be like to live as one of these creatures with whom he had peopled planet earth – as, in fairy stories, a king might dress up as a beggar just to savour life in the raw. Such a suggestion fails on two counts:

Firstly, it suggests a trivial purpose for the Incarnation whereas the New Testament regards Jesus' work with the utmost seriousness. This note of lofty seriousness is found in the birth narratives, in the 'successful' days in Galilee, and in the brief period of betrayal and death in Jerusalem. Far from the Incarnation providing God with a little playful diversion, it was costly: and if the experience of Gethsemane and Calvary are our measure, it was costly in the extreme.

Secondly, it suggests that God *could be* enriched, which is highly questionable and certainly might be thought to throw doubt on his perfection. Moreover, it suggests that *man* could be the source of this enrichment. Surely this presupposes too little about God and too much about man! God enriches himself, certainly: but always from within his own being. What he creates he creates not to be enriched *by*, but for himself to enrich. Far from God being enlarged by the experience of Incarnation he was impoverished by it. For whatever is meant precisely in Philippians 2.7, the passage certainly speaks of loss rather than of gain. Jesus beggared himself, took a lowly place, was subject to the vicissitudes of human life, endured all the trauma of death, found himself (in loyalty to his Father) at odds with his fellows, misunderstood even by those closest to him and betrayed by his chosen companions. There is no material here with which to build the thesis that the Incarnation took place for God's benefit.

2. *God revealed in man*

In Jesus, God revealed himself as never before and as nowhere else. To be sure, according to the Bible God revealed himself 'in many and various ways' (Hebrews 1.1) but it was always fragmentary and provisional. In Jesus, God disclosed himself personally and definitively.

There is a problem about God's self-revelation. If he were to show himself to us in all his glory we would be overwhelmed, stunned and deprived of any capacity freely and personally to respond (think of the disciples at the Transfiguration of Jesus who nearly went out of their minds because there was too much light). Because of this, God always shows himself in disguise or with a veil upon himself. He conceals himself even in the very act of revealing himself.

The Incarnation was no exception. In one sense Jesus is *not* what God is like – God is *not* a carpenter with rough hands and a Galilean accent. Jesus is God in disguise. It is not unlike the prophets of old who spoke in their own inadequate and culturally-conditioned words and yet, because they believed God took up those words, they could say 'thus saith the Lord'. So also Jesus, though he veils the naked truth of God, nevertheless *is* God revealing himself! His disguise is also his disclosure.

By becoming man, God revealed himself in a form that we can appreciate. He became a kind of enacted parable before our eyes. Jesus' parables put the deep things of God in earthly images – 'the Kingdom of God is like a grain of mustard seed'. That is how God accommodates his teaching to our hearing. Similarly, since God's sublime being is far beyond our comprehension, God accommodated himself to our capacities and stood before us as a man, a brother.

Of course, the event in which God revealed himself explicitly (in Jesus) is now past: it is finished (John 19.30). And yet, unlike other past occurrences in our history, this event is not over and done with. It is recapitulated in the believing community; where two or three are gathered together in Jesus' name, where the biblical witness to him is read and proclaimed, where his sacraments are celebrated, there Jesus is present and God's revelation in him is renewed. Jesus is for all times and for all peoples the 'place' of God's self-disclosure. He has been 'lifted up' to draw all men to himself (John 12.32).

3. *God on man's side*

Left to his own devices man is often like a blind person in a dark room; bewildered and lonely. Not unnaturally he complains that life is unfair – why should he suffer this lonely and perplexing lot? In the Incarnation, God sympathizes with man in his plight. He shares man's lot. No longer can we complain that God has no idea what it is like to be born, to grow, to live and to die because God knows fully what it is like (Hebrews 4.15).

Moreover, in sharing our lot, God in no way skated over the surface of our humanity, tasting it at select points where it might be considered not too bad – like a visiting dignitary being shown only the acceptable places and people. In the Incarnation God experienced the joy, the delight, the beauty of life; but, especially, he placed himself at the point of pain and shared in the harsh side of living and dying. He touched the raw edges of life, tasted its humiliations and frustrations; he experienced disappointments and failures and he went his lonely way to death. He even tasted (to the full) the bitter sense of desolation when a man can only cry out 'My God, why hast thou forsaken me' (Mark 15.34).

In the Incarnation we see no pampered Son shielded from the harsh realities but one who *as the beloved Son* allowed himself to become the outcast, rejected and forsaken. He knows, therefore, the plight of every lonely and pained, bewildered and betrayed person. To every man it can be said 'God hears thy sighs and counts thy tears' because in the days of his earthly life he, too, sighed and wept with the anguish of living and dying.

A further step. In the Incarnation God does more than sympathize with us, asuring us that he knows what it is like. He guarantees, through the Incarnation, that in all our joys and pains we are not alone: we are never forsaken. Whenever we say 'man' we must also say 'God' for man is nevermore 'lonely man' but always 'God's man', man claimed by God and man taken up by God into himself. There are, of course, many who *feel* lonely; but no people who *are* lonely, for 'Emmanuel: God is with us'.

Of course, mankind for the most part is unaware of this sublime truth and continues to bear its burden of cares as though all alone. But whether he knows it or not, the Incarnation means that man is never bereft of God. There is no such thing as a 'godless world', there is only a world that does not yet fully know that God is with it.

4. *Humanity taken into God*

Without the Incarnation God is Father, Son and Holy Spirit. As a result of the Incarnation God is Father, Son, Holy Spirit *and man.* (We must add that this 'result' extends backwards as well as forwards, so that there never was a time when it was otherwise: compare the expression in Revelation 13.8 'the Lamb slain from the foundation of the world'.) Man exists in the very heart of God, caught up in that form of God's being to which we give the name 'Son'.

This is surely what makes the Incarnation such a vital and exciting belief. God has in store for his creature an almost inconceivable destiny, that he should participate in the very being of God. If we might think of God's dynamic, Trinitarian life as a kind of festive dance, then man is taken by the hand and brought into the moving circle.

The mechanics of this defy understanding, but perhaps the idea of an exchange helps. Paul expressed this succinctly in writing to the Corinthians: 'For you know the grace of our Lord Jesus Christ, that though he was rich, yet for your sakes he became poor, so that by his poverty you might become rich' (2 Corinthians 8.9). A similar thought is found in Athanasius, an early champion of right Christian belief who, writing about the Incarnation, said 'For the Word, perceiving that no otherwise could the corruption of men be undone save by death as a necessary condition . . . takes to himself a body capable of death, that it, by partaking of the Word who is above all, might be worthy to die in the stead of all, and might, because of the Word which was come to dwell in it, remain incorruptible, and that henceforth corruption might be stayed from all by the Grace of the Resurrection' – which is simply a longer way of saying that through the Incarnation Jesus suffered and we benefitted: he became poor and we were enriched.

5. *A sacrament of renewal*

The major sacraments of the church – baptism and holy communion – use ordinary things to communicate spiritual realities (so the old Prayer Book catechism: 'what meanest thou by this word Sacrament?' 'I mean an outward and visible sign of an inward and spiritual grace

. . .'). The water of baptism and the bread of eucharist speak to us of 'water of life' and 'bread of life'. They are, in Christian experience, powerful visual aids.

But they are more than this. God uses these signs not simply to teach us but to visit us: not simply to communicate a message but to share his presence. Through these ordinary, everyday things God enacts once again his name 'Emmanuel', 'God with us'. But where God is present, there 'salvation' is present: for God is always making things new. Where God is, there is new creation. He is constantly breaking down the old and inadequate and transforming it into the wholesome and life-giving.

The primary sacrament, however, is not baptism or communion but the flesh and blood of Jesus: his humanity. The carpenter of Nazareth is the symbol and vehicle of God's presence with man and of God's renewal of man which his presence entails. Hence the manhood of Jesus is, as it were, taken apart and re-made: it is put down and raised up, crucified and risen! This humanity and what befell it stands for all time and for all men as God's sure purpose: 'behold, I make all things new' (Revelation 21.5). What happened to Jesus' humanity is the promise of what must happen to us, too. As Simeon said of the baby (Luke 2.34) 'this child is set for the fall and rising of many . . . .' We, too, shall participate in the breaking down and the building up, in the dying and rising: 'for if we have been united with him in a death like his, we shall certainly be united with him in a resurrection like his' (Romans 6.5).

6. *A new pattern for living*
Jesus took our humanity but gave it a new shape and a new life-style. In doing so he left us an example to follow (1 Peter 2.21).

(i) *The way of dependence.* Despite our gregariousness, we are for the most part fiercely independent. Even in small things man finds it hard to be in someone's debt or to accept something as an unmerited gift. We wish to stand on our own feet, making our own decisions; we want to be 'self-made' men and women. Yet in this determination lies the seed of our own discomfiture, because we cannot sustain ourselves. In the celebrated phrase 'no man is an island unto himself' and we depend on others throughout our lives and, ultimately, we depend on God. It is odd that we so persistently rebel against this condition of dependence and recklessly strive to go it alone.

Jesus embraced dependence. He volunteered to enter the world as a helpless baby very much in the hands of other people. He lived in the mutual interdependence of family and social life without rebellion. He put his destiny in the hands of fickle followers and jealous leaders. He lived out of the hand of God without complaint.

We think of such dependence as involving high risk. Certainly Jesus was let down, betrayed, abandoned and killed off. But his resurrection guarantees that in real terms (we might also say in the long run) only the way of dependence can bring satisfaction and wholeness and life with God.

(ii) *The way of the cross.* Humanity seems to be convinced that something like the 'survival of the fittest' is the key to successful and satisfying life. In fact, the pursuit of this policy leads straight to the grave, for despite all the brute self-assertiveness of which man is capable everyone grows old, falls sick and dies.

Jesus sets before us (in statement: Mark 8.35, as well as in action) the policy of 'the survival of the weakest'. He lived without the trappings or the reality of power, without manipulating or coercing his fellows, without making demands on God. He let others dispose over him; he climbed down, let go, gave up and died – and, lo and behold, he lives for evermore! It was this startling reversal of what mankind regards as self-evident that led Paul to speak of God's weakness in terms of strength and to rejoice in his own weaknesses (see 1 Corinthians 1.25 and 2 Corinthians 12.9).

(iii) *The way of love.* 'Greater love has no man than this, that a man lay down his life for his friends' (John 15.13). It was not only on Calvary but throughout the course of his ministry and throughout the entire Incarnation that Jesus laid down his life for those whom he called his friends.

And all this for love! 'For God so loved the world that he gave . . . .' (John 3.16). It has rightly been said that if for the word 'love' in 1 Corinthians, chapter 13 you read 'Jesus' then you will have a correct description of God Incarnate. Here, to be sure, is the clue to it all. Jesus took humanity to display before us the life of love, life that counts others better than the self, life that puts the well-being of others before its own.

This pattern of living, the way of dependence, the way of the cross, the way of love, is splendidly captured in the well-known prayer of Francis of Assisi:

O divine Master, grant that I may not so much
seek to be consoled, as to console;
to be understood, as to understand;
to be loved, as to love;
for it is in giving that we receive,
it is in pardoning that we are pardoned,
and it is in dying that we are born
to Eternal Life.

3

'He died to save us all'

The Confirmation course was drawing to its close. The vicar had spoken at length about many things: the nature of Christian belief, the authority of the Bible, the duties of a churchman and the like. Now he wanted to be sure that everyone had understood, so he asked if there were any remaining questions or uncertainties. Somewhat diffidently one young man spoke up, 'I'm sorry, but I still don't understand why Jesus had to die. Can you explain it again?'

Such a young man speaks for many. At the heart of Christian faith and practice stands a strange event, the crucifixion; but it is far from clear why Jesus had to endure this ghastly fate. Why did Jesus die? It is to this question we must now turn.

TWO SORTS OF ANSWERS

In fact, there are two kinds of questions and two sorts of answers. If we ask 'Why did Jesus die?' we might be asking a question about the cause(s) of his death: what led up to it, who was responsible for it, what circumstances conspired to bring it about. This kind of question expects an answer beginning 'because. . .'. But, if we ask

'Why did Jesus die?' we might be asking a question about the purpose(s) of his death: what was it *for*, what (if anything) did it achieve, what resulted from it. This kind of question expects an answer beginning 'in order that. . .'. The Atonement really concerns this second kind of question and answer; it has to do with the purpose(s) of Jesus' death. However, it might help to note, briefly, the causes.

THE CAUSE OF JESUS' DEATH

1. *The Sanhedrin*, i.e. the ruling Council of the Jews. Though its members were devout people looking for the coming of God's rule, the Sanhedrin was antagonistic to Jesus. Perhaps it was his background that disturbed them; 'Can anything good come out of Nazareth?' said one genuine Israelite (John 1.46–47 and see John 7.41–42). Perhaps Jesus' indifference towards the many scruples of Jewish tradition offended; at times he bluntly criticized this tradition as confusing and oppressive (Mark 7.9–13, Matthew 23.4). Worse still, Jesus seemed at times to set himself above the holy law of Moses (Matthew 5.21). Perhaps Jesus' popularity with the crowds irritated leaders who apparently 'loved the place of honour in the synagogues, and salutations in the market places' (Matthew 23.6–7). Maybe it was the threat Jesus posed to the *status quo* that they most feared; 'If we let him go on thus, everyone will believe in him, and the Romans will come and destroy both our holy place and our nation' (John 11.48).

Whatever the reasons, the religious authorities showed signs of unease from early in Jesus' ministry and already in Mark 3.6 we learn that the Pharisees 'held council with the Herodians against him, how to destroy him'.

2. *Pilate*, the Roman governor. At this point in their history, the Jewish people probably had no authority to execute offenders. In any case, it suited the purpose of the leaders to have Pilate execute Jesus (so that any future blame might attach to Rome rather than to themselves!) in order that Jesus might be killed by crucifixion (never a Jewish form of punishment) and be accounted cursed by God (see Deuteronomy 21.23).

Pilate might have resisted. Indeed, the records show that he made some efforts to secure Jesus' release. But Rome tended to post to Palestine its weaker officials and in practice Pilate was simply manipulated by the Sanhedrin and he allowed Jesus, whom he recognized as innocent, to be executed. The ground on which the Sanhedrin had condemned Jesus was that of blasphemy (he, a mere man, claimed to be equal with God: Mark 14.61–63, John 5.18). This would not have interested Pilate; the charge put to him was that Jesus was an insurrectionist, a pretender king.

3. *Judas*, one of the Twelve. The Jewish authorities could have engineered Jesus' death without Judas' help, but his offer aided their scheme. They had decided to do nothing during the festive season of Passover because Jesus was something of a popular hero and his arrest would cause a public outcry. But Judas agreed to lead them to the hideaway where Jesus disappeared each evening after the day's public events. In this way the authorities were able to bring their plans forward and take Jesus by stealth without any crowd disorder.

What was Judas' motive? Perhaps he was afraid and supposed that by turning king's evidence he might save his own life. Perhaps he was a Zealot (a political revolutionary) who thought it was high time Jesus acted, and believed that by arranging Jesus' arrest he would force decisive action. Perhaps he was simply greedy and betrayed Jesus for the money.

It is significant that Judas was 'one of the Twelve'. Ancient Israel – God's own people – had proved repeatedly faithless. Now, God's son is handed over by one of the chosen band; treachery comes from within the elect. And though Judas alone betrayed Jesus, the other apostles were little better for 'they all forsook him and fled'.

4. *Satan*, power of evil. In the Old Testament (Job 1.6ff. for example) 'Satan' can simply mean 'the Tester'; one who puts a man through his paces to see if he will prove faithful. But in the New Testament 'Satan' is one of a variety of terms used to describe forces hostile to God and to men. 'Satan' was at work in the events leading to Jesus' death.

We do not need to repeat the biblical *terms* ('evil spirits', 'Satan', 'prince of demons', etc.) but we should not lightly jettison the biblical *ideas*. Here the idea is that Jesus' ministry involved a conflict between God working in him and evil forces active in the world. (The exorcisms in particular are regarded as signs of God's victorious opposition to such forces: Matthew 12.28.) Jesus' death-his apparent downfall – was at the same time the culmination of this conflict and the decisive defeat of the power of evil.

5. *God*, sovereign over all. God was responsible for the death of Jesus! This has to be said even though others, already mentioned, retain their responsibility. In speaking of his impending suffering and death, Jesus declares 'it is necessary . . ', a characteristic round-about way of saying 'God requires and ordains it'. During his trial Jesus assures Pilate, 'you would have no power over me unless it had been given you from above' (John 19.11) and in a debate with Peter he says, 'Do you think that I cannot appeal to my Father, and he will at once send me more than twelve legions of angels? But how then should the scriptures be fulfilled, that it must be so?' (Matthew 26.53–54). In his first 'sermon' Peter declares that Jesus was indeed crucified 'by the hands of lawless men' but that he was 'delivered up according to the definite plan and foreknowledge of God' (Acts 2.23). So, strange as it seems, Jesus' death was part of God's intention.

Here, then, are the causes of Jesus' death. We must now ask, 'What did Jesus' death accomplish and what was it for?'.

THE PURPOSE OF JESUS' DEATH

The Bible gives us no simple answer to our question. Instead it makes a number of bold affirmations which it leaves us to elucidate – which is why the Church has struggled through the centuries to understand the Atonement. 'Christ died for our sins', 'Christ died according to the scriptures', 'Christ our Passover is sacrificed for us', 'being justified by his death. . .': what do such statements really mean? How did the death of this particular man, Jesus of Nazareth, make any difference to God or to the world or to me?

For convenience we shall consider Jesus' death under three headings: 1. Jesus' death and forgiveness; 2. Jesus' death and reconciliation; 3. Jesus' death and new creation. In each section we shall begin with a look at certain presuppositions and at some insights from the Bible.

1. FORGIVENESS

'Christ died for our sins' (1 Corinthians 15.3) 'Let it be known to you . . . that through this man forgiveness of sins is proclaimed to you' (Acts 13.38). If we are to appreciate what is meant here we must note three presuppositions:

(a) *Man is a sinner*. The Bible speaks of sin in a number of ways. Sin means *deviation* from the right path; just as an archer might aim at a target but miss, so man misses the target of right behaviour. Instead of heading straight he deviates and wanders in byways, distracted. Sin is *failure* to fulfil obligations: man has the duty to live uprightly and is guilty of neglecting this task. Instead of faithfully discharging his responsibilities he recklessly ignores them. Sin is *rebellion*; not simply turning against a friend but turning against a superior to whom loyalty is due. It is akin to mutiny by soldiers or like a son turning against his father. Sin is a kind of *rottenness*; all may look fine on the surface but there is corruption within.

According to the Bible (and authenticated in human experience) sin is universal: 'all have sinned and fall short of the glory of God' (Romans 3.23). One way of depicting this is given in the story of man's primeval 'fall' in Genesis chapter 3, a story to which Paul refers when he says 'as sin came into the world through one man' (Romans 5.12) and 'as in Adam all die' (1 Corinthians 15.22). We can accept the point of the story without necessarily regarding it as literal history.

(b) *God is holy*. Some of the 'gods' to whom men have bowed down (and still bow) behave little better than ourselves! But the God to whom the Bible points us is pure perfection: he is holy. In its earlier connotations in Israel, 'holy' meant simply 'separated', i.e. someone or something given over to God for sacred purposes (e.g. priests or Temple). But ethical associations soon gathered around the word and 'holy' came to denote someone whose being and behaviour are beyond all reproach. Isaiah regularly speaks of God as 'the Holy One of Israel'.

Because God is holy he requires his creatures also to be holy (Leviticus 19.2). How could God be satisfied with anything less? But God not only intends man for holiness: he is wholly displeased at man's failure to attain it. This holy God is appalled at man's sin and (so to speak) recoils in horror at it ('thou art of purer eyes than to behold evil, and canst not look on wrong' (Habakkuk 1.1)). So God opposes man's sin with divine displeasure, with judgement and condemnation.

(c) *God is committed to man.* Although God is fiercely opposed to man's *sin*, he is deeply concerned for *man.* It is not enough, therefore, for God simply to respond to human sin by, for instance, destroying man and the entire sinful world – the ancient story of the Flood is intended to show that such an idea had occurred to the Almighty but had been rejected. It belongs to God to find some way of overcoming the effects of sin without annihilating man; of establishing some way by which sin might be forgiven.

We might almost say that there is a kind of dilemma within God, or at any rate what would prove a dilemma for us! In his commitment to man God determines to forgive him and certainly will not abandon or destroy him; yet in his holiness God cannot ignore man's sin or simply turn a blind eye to it. Hence the prophet's picture of God pleading with man to give up the evil ways that lead inevitably to death: 'Why will you die, O house of Israel? For I have no pleasure in the death of anyone, says the Lord God, so turn and live' (Ezekiel 18.31–32).

How, then, might God forgive sin and restore the sinner?

The way of repentance

The prophet calls sinful man to 'turn and live'. Such a change of heart (change in attitudes and disposition) leads to change in behaviour. And whereas God opposes sinful man, he accepts the humble and contrite (see e.g. Psalm 51.17). However, there are two difficulties here.

The first is that sinful man is unable wholly to repent. He might wish to improve; he might be sorry for his wrongdoing; he might indeed 'turn' on many occasions. But a deep-seated and permanent repentance seems to be beyond man's capacity to achieve. Man might as well try to regenerate damaged brain tissues as create for himself 'a new heart' altogether intent on obedience.

Jesus, however, is the perfect penitent. He is altogether without sin (see John 8.46, Hebrews 4.15, 1 Peter 2.22) and is wholly pleasing to God. Even so, he does not 'trade' on this perfection but humbles himself before God, takes his stand with sinful men and is baptized with John's 'baptism of repentance for the forgiveness of sins' (Mark 1.4). This baptism is only an anticipation of his real 'baptism' on Calvary which he experienced with similar humble obedience. He is, as it were, penitent on our behalf; he acknowledges sin that was not his own and repents for us.

The second problem is that even the finest repentance cannot undo the wrong that has been committed. Repentance regrets the wrong and determines never to repeat it; but the wrong is not effaced. However impassioned the plea ('Out, out, damned spot'!) the stain of sin remains. Some objective act is required which 'atones' for the wrong, that is to say something that makes amends for it. 'Repent . . . that your sins may be blotted out' (Acts 3.19) can only be said where such an objective act is presupposed (namely, 'what God foretold by the mouth of all the prophets, that his Christ should suffer. . .'(Acts 3.18)).

Jesus makes amends. He is the perfect reparation for damage done. In his perfect being, in his obedient life and in his humble death, God finds a man who is wholly pleasing and with whom he can be utterly satisfied. 'This is my beloved Son with whom I am well pleased' (Matthew 3.17).

Difficulties remain. How can the repentance of one man have relevance for someone else? How can the obedience of one make up for the sin of another? To some extent these difficulties are resolved when we take seriously the nature of the 'one man' in question because (as we shall see) Jesus is regarded in the New Testament as nothing less than 'representative man'. To this theme we must return shortly.

The way of sacrifice

The origins of animal sacrifice are shrouded in the hidden past of Israel and of her neighbours. At some stage the slaughter and burning of an animal was supposed to foster (or at least to represent) communion between the worshipper and his god. Later, sacrifice was thought to have specifically atoning significance, that is to say it was deemed to help in wiping out sin. Within Israel there were various kinds of sacrifice ('burnt-offerings and oblations', peace-offerings, sin and guilt-offerings and the like) and carefully organized rituals were developed as well as a priestly class whose job it was to offer sacrifices.

Of course, animal sacrifices had severe limitations. Israel's religious leaders knew well that the mere slaughter of an animal could not really overcome the consequences of man's sin; the priest, the worshipper and the beast itself were all part of the sinful scene! Nevertheless the sacrificial system witnessed to the need for some objective offering to be made to God whereby his offended holiness might be satisfied; compensation, so to speak, must be paid. Sacrifice pointed in this direction but was powerless to provide the offering needed.

Jesus is the perfect offering. That is why the New Testament uses sacrificial language about him: 'Behold the Lamb of God who takes away the sin of the world' (John 1.29), 'Christ, our Paschal lamb, has been sacrificed' (1 Corinthians 5.7), 'But when Christ appeared as a high priest of the good things that have come . . . he entered once for all into the Holy Place, taking not the blood of goats and calves but his own blood' (Hebrews 9.11–12). This man's priesthood is sinless and this man's offering is altogether able to atone because it is utterly without spot or blemish.

Here, then, is suggestive imagery. But we must be careful in exploring it to avoid any thought of God being irrationally wrathful or any thought of Jesus 'buttering him up'! Here, too, the realization that Jesus is 'representative man' will help us to avoid most dangers.

The way of justification

Paul explores a different approach. He envisages a law court. God is the judge and man the accused. Man inevitably receives the sentence of condemnation, 'guilty'. Yet man longs for a better verdict; God also desires this. How might a favourable verdict be secured? Jesus, the judge, stands in man's place and bears the 'guilty' verdict that should be pronounced on us so that, as a result, we receive the 'not guilty' ('justified') verdict that should have been spoken to him.

This, at any rate, is how a number of Christians interpret Paul's legal terminology. There are, however, severe problems with this reconstruction and many scholars think that Paul's meaning is rather different. The problems are:

(i) insofar as man (on Paul's own admission: see Romans 7) is not altogether free, and certainly is not free to choose whether to be a sinner or not, how far is it really proper for man to be arraigned before God at all? Can man not rightly plead diminished responsibility?

(ii) insofar as God must act justly, how can he be content that another man steps forward into the place of the accused? Some suggest that this difficulty is minimal because in ordinary life we allow someone else to pay a prisoner's fine – and, in any case (they say) we are thinking of the Judge (Jesus) placing himself in the dock and taking the prisoner's punishment. The difficulty remains, however; for we are not speaking of a fine but of a death sentence and in what court of justice would it be allowed for an innocent man (even the judge himself), to be executed in place of the guilty prisoner?

(iii) insofar as someone else is substituted for the prisoner (Jesus is declared 'guilty') how can this really divert onto the rest of mankind the verdict that rightfully belonged to him ('not guilty')?

The accusation that some kind of legal fiction is involved is hard to resist. The clue, surely, lies in the nature of Jesus (to which we have already referred) as 'representative man'. It is time to pay some attention to this.

Jesus, representative man

In the New Testament Jesus is certainly an individual person living at a particular time and place. He is 'Jesus of Nazareth'.

At the same time he is more than this. He is 'Son of Man' which, amongst other things, means that he is one who represents the 'saints of the Most High' (Daniel 7.13–18). As such a representative, Paul compares him with Adam: 'as in Adam . . . so in Christ'. It is of no fundamental importance here whether Adam was (or was thought to be) an *historical* figure; what matters is that he was regarded as a *corporate* figure. The corporate character of Jesus comes out in a striking passage where Paul says 'we are convinced that one has died for all'; we expect him then to say 'therefore all others need not die', instead of which he writes 'therefore all have died' (2 Corinthians 5.14). This conclusion is possible only because for Paul Jesus was one in whom (all) others are somehow summed up. (That is why Paul also wrote, 'even though we once regarded Jesus from a human point of view, we regard him thus no longer' (2 Corinthians 5.16).) Perhaps it is in his letter to the Colossians that Paul expresses this most clearly: Jesus is (a) the one in whom God's being is present, (b) the one through whom all things were created and are now sustained, and (c) the one in whom all things 'whether on earth or in heaven' are reconciled to God (see Colossians 1.15–20).

Because Jesus is our representative and somehow contains us within himself certain difficulties we have noted in passing are (partially at least) resolved. He is the perfect penitent; but he is this not only *for* me but *as myself* – it is 'I (who) have been crucified with Christ' so that 'it is no longer I who live but Christ lives in me' (Galatians 2.20, see also Colossians 3.3). His sacrifice of himself to God (wholly acceptable because without blemish) is *my offering*; he does not offer himself *instead of* me but *as myself*, bearing my name. He stands in court not as a substitute prisoner – as though this could ever be tolerated – but *as myself*! The verdict 'guilty' is also pronounced on us (in him) and we are raised up with Christ into (as Paul puts it) the 'heavenly places' (Ephesians 1.3). Now we can see why Paul urges us to identify both with Christ's death and with his resurrection for his death was *our* death and his resurrection *our* glorification. Such is the nature of Jesus our representative.

Because we are 'incorporate' in him, what properly should only be said of him can also be said of us, and vice-versa. Clearly he (as God) is rich and we (as sinners) are poor: but it can also be said that he is poor and we rich (see 2 Corinthians 8.9).

So forgiveness is achieved because Christ our representative dies, as must befall sinful man; and he rises, as is proper for man without sin. But there is another way of considering the purpose of Jesus' death, not so much in terms of forgiveness as of reconciliation.

2. RECONCILIATION

'God was in Christ reconciling the world to himself' (2 Corinthians 5.19). 'Reconciliation' speaks directly to us today (perhaps more so than 'sin' and 'forgiveness') partly because the behavioural sciences feature so prominently, and partly because broken relationships are, tragically, so common. If we explore the meaning of Jesus' death in terms of reconciliation we must again note certain presuppositions.

(a) *Man is made for relationship.* The principle 'it is not good that man should be alone' (Genesis 2.18) is, perhaps, already a hint that man is made for partnership – not simply for lateral relationships within family or society but for relationship with God. Augustine's celebrated saying is right: 'O God, thou hast made man for thyself and our hearts are restless 'til they find their rest in thee'. God made the universe to enjoy relationship with himself and in calling Israel into a special partnership he was not turning away from the rest of creation but advancing his purposes which would eventually embrace all men (see e.g. Isaiah 49.6).

(b) *Relationship has been broken.* The intended relationship has broken down because God's chosen partner has proved faithless. The man intended by God to saunter through his garden after dinner in pleasant conversation with God, now hides himself 'because he is afraid' (Genesis 3.8–10). Israel, chosen by God to enjoy harmonious fellowship with himself, wanders off after other gods. Because the intended relationship is broken, God's dealings with his partner now take on a threatening quality; man is ejected from the garden: Israel is sent into exile. God is not unfaithful to his estranged partner but he can only relate now in judgement instead of grace – or, rather, his grace now meets the estranged partner in the form of uncomfortable judgement instead of in the form of comforting love.

(c) *God will restore relationship.* The situation is intolerable, for God and not simply for man! It is as though a beloved bride had committed adultery or a dear son had abandoned the home. Something of the sorrow and anguish of the grieved partner comes out in Hosea's message: 'How can I give you up, O Ephraim! How can I hand you over, O Israel! How can I make you like Admah! How can I treat you like Zeborim! My heart recoils within me, my compassion grows warm and tender' (Hosea 11.8). The possibility that God might simply abandon faithless man is ruled out by the nature of God as utterly loyal to his purposes and to himself – 'if we are faithless, he remains faithful' (2 Timothy 2.13).

How, then, might God reconcile man and restore the broken relationship?

Through redemption

We may think of an object pawned in a moment of need but later to be bought back ('redeemed'). Or we may think of someone (in a society other than ours) sold into slavery or taken prisoner in war and able, at a price, to be freed ('redeemed'). In Old Testament times it quite easily happened that someone would be enslaved or captured and it then fell to that person's next-of-kin to secure his release by paying the necessary ransom price. In this way the relative became his 'redeemer'.

Israel, God's chosen people, became enslaved by false gods and false securities; enticed away she became faithless. God will act as her next-of-kin and will redeem her! Mankind as a whole has become captive, 'sold under sin' as Paul puts it (Romans 7.14) but God will free him, release him from prison and bring him home!

So Jesus spoke of his purpose like this: 'the Son of Man came not to be served but to serve, and to give his life as a ransom for many' (Mark 10.45) – 'ransom' being, of course, the price paid in order to redeem 'the many'. Similarly Paul says of Christians that they were 'bought with a price' (1 Corinthians 6.20, see also Act 20.28). Who, after all, was able to pay the kind of price that redemption of the universe demanded? How, from within the created order, might the price be found? Jesus, the God-made-man, is himself the price. Being himself God, no higher sum could be conceived.

The New Testament does not develop this thought further. Some early Christian writers rashly suggested that God paid the ransom to the devil, as though God were beholden to him! 'They speculated that God had laid a trap for the devil. He had made a bargain with him in order to ensnare him. Christ had been the bait. God had offered the devil power over his Son if he would let humanity go free. The offer had been greedily accepted, for it had appealed to the evil one's inordinate pride. But having let go of humanity to lay hold of Christ, the devil found he had been duped and caught. . . For he could not hold Christ, who was sinless' (R. Wallace, *The Atoning Death of Christ*, p. 70, Marshall, Morgan & Scott). Such speculation is quite out of order. We simply cannot ask 'to whom was the ransom paid?'; and if we were to ask this, it would most certainly be improper to answer 'it was paid to the devil' for God is in no sense obliged, able or willing to make deals with forces of evil.

Through peace

A broken relationship means a turbulent relationship; squabbling, friction and dis-ease. Because man is out of harmony with God he encounters a whole range of misfortunes including sickness, pain and death. Man is at war within himself and with his environment because he is at enmity with God.

Jesus establishes peace. Not only is a temporary or patchy truce called, but a unilateral declaration is made that hostilities have ended. How is this peace established? We have only isolated clues.

Firstly, throughout Jesus' life there is no rebellion against God. Even in Gethsemane and on Calvary he is willing to do what God requires. To him God can indeed say 'my beloved Son in whom I am well pleased' and he, in turn, can say to the Father 'not my will but thine be done'. No longer does man wish to assert himself or usurp the prerogative of God. The rebellious pattern of Genesis chapter 3 is reversed in the obedient pattern of Philippians 2.6–11.

Secondly, in Jesus' own person – since he is God and man – a new harmony or relationship of the most intimate kind is set up (see further the previous chapter *Jesus, God and man).* When we associate with this thought the view that Jesus is representative man, we see how this peace is really *ours.* That is why Jesus not only used the characteristic Jewish greeting 'Shalom' ('peace') but *gave* peace (a new kind of peace: John 14.27).

So Paul speaks of 'the gospel of peace' and affirms that Christ not only brings 'peace with God' (Romans 5.1) but enables harmony amongst disparate peoples (Ephesians 2.14). The ancient promise is fulfilled: 'speak tenderly to Jerusalem, and cry to her that her warfare is ended' (Isaiah 40.2).

Through covenant

The relationship was not accidental or casual; it was begun by covenant. God pledged himself to creation, to Noah, to Abraham, to Israel. Each time covenant was seriously broken, God reaffirmed it or established a fresh one.

Jeremiah foretold a new covenant (Jeremiah 31.31) qualitatively better than all previous ones because this (he said) would go to the heart of things. Jesus' death ratifies this new covenant between God and man (Hebrews 9.15–22 reminds us that any covenant must be ratified in blood). Hence, at his farewell supper, he offers his followers tokens of this with the words, 'this is my blood of the new covenant' (Mark 14.24). Here is an agreement between God and man signed, sealed, delivered and eternally binding.

What makes it qualitatively better than previous covenants? This covenant, for the first time, is made by two partners both of whom will stand by their word without the slightest possibility of equivocation. Now, not only will *God* be faithful to man, but *man* (in Jesus) will be faithful to God also. This (representative) man will not fail.

So reconciliation is established between God and man through Jesus. There remains a further way of considering the purpose of Jesus' death; in terms of new creation.

3. NEW CREATION

Man is sinful and needs pardon; man is estranged and needs to be reconciled. But man is also incomplete and inadequate and needs renewal. If you like, evolution needs to take a significant step forward! Once again we must notice certain presuppositions if we are to appreciate this thought.

(a) *Man is incomplete.* It is as though each one of us has some inbuilt flaw. We are not as God wills us to be; we are frail and vulnerable. To be sure, the more we investigate man, the more amazed we are at the complexity and subtlety of his composition – we are indeed 'fearfully and wonderfully made'! At the same time we are all, more or less, conscious of the severe limitations of our being; the finitude of our minds, the susceptibility of our bodies, the fickleness of our moods, the transience of our stay in life. Man lives dangerously in a difficult and unobliging world and is himself inadequate to the demands made upon him.

(b) *Man is destined to die*. The greatest strength, the most astonishing capacity of mind or spirit, all eventually disintegrates, falls sick, dies. And our knowledge of impending death colours all our living to some extent mocking our every attainment. Even whilst we live, sickness often assails us and a sense of futility is never far away. No wonder Paul speaks of death as 'the last enemy' to be overcome!

(c) *God determines that man shall live*. It is not God's will that we should be incomplete and hopelessly inadequate; he destines us for perfection. 'For he has made known to us the mystery of his will, according to his purpose which he set forth in Christ, as a plan for the fullness of time, to unite all things in him, things in heaven and things on earth' (Ephesians 1.9–10). This is a perfection which will embrace the entire world – such is, for example, the vision of that strange book with which the Bible ends: 'I saw a new heaven and a new earth: for the first heaven and the first earth had passed away' (Revelation 21.1): 'And he who sat upon the throne said, "Behold, I make all things new" ' (Revelation 21.5). God will come to man's aid and re-create him so that he may truly live.

How, then, will God renew man in the perfection he intends?

By means of example

Jesus sets before us in the pattern of his living and dying a new, perfected creation. He is, therefore, our example (John 13.15, 1 Peter 2.21). His way of living (and dying) was radically different from ours. The principle of his way is set out in Mark 8.35, 'whoever would save his life will lose it; and whoever loses his life for my sake and the gospel's will find it. . .'.

Here we encounter a sharp criticism of our life-style. Ours we may call, not unfairly, the way of 'the survival of the fittest'. For we struggle and strive, we assert ourselves, we impress our importance upon ourselves (and, so far as we can, upon others) yet, bitter though it is, all this assertion cannot save us from the grave – 'I say, "You are gods . . . nevertheless, you shall die like men" ' (Psalm 82.6–7). So 'survival of the fittest' is no real survival at all, only the constant round of living leading to dying.

Jesus' policy we might call 'the survival of the weakest' for he abandons all attempt at self-assertion, all effort at imposing himself on others, all striving to secure his destiny; instead he lets go of every claim, lets go even of himself, is subordinate, is at the disposal of others; he is content to be a servant, to be obedient, to die. This way also leads to the grave; but, astonishing though it seems, it leads *through* the grave and (if we may so express it) out the other side. The guarantee of this is that Jesus, who followed this policy to its bitter end, actually was raised from death to life and now lives 'at God's right hand', that is in perfection and power.

This is the example which Jesus sets out before us. To follow this example is to follow Jesus through death and into life – 'he who believes in me, though he die yet shall he live. . .' (John 11.25).

By means of death

We might prefer God to superimpose a perfected manhood upon our old, frail and flawed humanity (compare Paul's wish in 2 Corinthians 5.4). God will not do this. He unmakes the old in order to make it anew. Therefore before man can be given God's intended perfection he has to be put down in death. God's satisfaction with his planned perfection involves a severe judgement on man's inadequate condition. God is *against* man as he now is, just as truly as God is *for* man as he will become. It might even be said that man as he now is is under God's 'curse', the curse of God's judgement.

Jesus takes this dissatisfaction of God upon himself; he becomes a 'cursed thing' in our place (again, as representative man embracing us all in himself). This is precisely what Paul affirms in 2 Corinthians 5.21 and Galatians 3.13 (alluding to Deuteronomy 21.23). 'Jesus experiences death, not as one who is at least inwardly sustained by God's miraculous protection, but as one who is abandoned by God to the derision of his enemies, so that out of the darkness which engulfs him he can only cry to God: "My God, my God, why hast thou forsaken me?" Inconceivable though it may appear, he experiences death as one of the many who have fallen victim to corruption. He has taken our place' (*Theological Dictionary of the New Testament*, Vol. IV, p.343, Eerdmans SCM Press). God makes no easy compromise with the old in bringing the new into being.

By means of life

Jesus told Nicodemus, a leading light of his day, 'Truly, truly, I say to you, unless one is born anew, he cannot see the kingdom of God' (John 3.3). Nicodemus was astonished, utterly failing to comprehend. Paul also wrote of this new 'birth', 'if any one is in Christ, he is a new creation; the old has passed away, behold the new has come' (2 Corinthians 5.17). Of course, the new creation *is* Jesus. He is the man who shares the very life of God himself; whose life, therefore, even though it is for a moment snuffed out, can never finally be extinguished. His humanity is infused with divine life and is caught up in God's being.

Once again, if we are to appreciate what this means for us we must take note that Jesus is representative man, the one in whom others are embraced. His new manhood, therefore, is *my* new manhood.

YESTERDAY, TODAY AND FOR EVER

The great umbrella term for God's atoning work in Jesus is 'salvation'. The root meaning of this word is 'space'; space to live, room to breathe, freedom to be myself and to 'do my own thing'. It later came to mean victory in battle, victory through which an oppressed individual or nation is rescued and vindicated. To some extent, the provision of a king over Israel (ambiguously interpreted in the Old Testament) represented God's determination to lead and safeguard his people. But the monarch proved unworthy and there grew up the confident expectation that one day God would provide a new king ('great David's greater son') who would truly save his people. God has done this in Jesus. Matthew records the angelic promise that Jesus 'will save his people from their sins' (Matthew 1.21) and in Luke's gospel Jesus sums up his mission as 'to seek and to save that which is lost'(Luke 19.10). 'Saviour' quickly became amongst the early Christians a common term for Jesus.

Everyone knows the story of the keen young lass who asked a bishop 'Are you saved?' to which he replied, in effect: 'If you mean "Have I been saved?" the answer is "Yes I trust so, through Christ's death": if you mean "Am I being saved?" the answer is "I believe so, through the work of God's Holy Spirit": and if you mean "Shall I be saved?" the answer is "I hope so, when Jesus returns as judge" '. We may consider the three tenses of salvation in connection with forgiveness, reconciliation and new creation and also in relation to Paul's famous trilogy 'faith, hope and love'.

There is a backward thrust to salvation and it concerns, primarily, the forgiveness of sin. This forgiveness was achieved by Christ's death and resurrection and we reach back to this event in faith. It is by faith we are saved. The gospel is good news of a victory already accomplished; faith is an echo of Jesus' cry 'it is finished' (John 19.30).

There is a present aspect to salvation and it concerns, primarily, reconciliation and the restoration of fellowship with God. This reconciliation was achieved by Christ's death and resurrection and we accept and express this fellowship in love. 'God is love' (1 John 4.8), so that to be in harmony with God, to participate in fellowship with him, is to live in love: 'he who loves is born of God and knows God. He who does not love does not know God' (1 John 4.7–8). Love is the characteristic of reconciliation with God and with one another.

There is a forward look to salvation and it concerns, primarily, new creation and the disclosure of perfection 'in Christ'. This new creation was brought into being by Christ's death and resurrection and we reach towards it in hope. For the moment it is hidden from us; it awaits us up ahead. It is an 'inheritance which is imperishable, undefiled and unfading, kept in heaven for you' (1 Peter 1.4). Christ's new life is the guarantee that our hope will not be disappointed. Hope, by definition, does not yet possess what is hoped for: but it waits for it with patience, aware that 'in this hope we were saved' (Romans 8.24).

Atonement is God's work of forgiveness, of reconciliation and of renewal, and man is summoned to respond to this work in faith, in love and in hope.

Index of Names and Subjects

Index of Biblical References